FARM GIRL
meditations

31 Days to Love the Life You Live

❧

Holly Love King

Cover Artist: Emily Wright
Contributing Interior Artist: Kevin Faulkner

TO FARM BOY

Thank you for moving us to the country
so I could live out my days as your Farm Girl.
For helping every one of my dreams
come true, from barns to books.
You are just as I wished.

❧ CONTENTS ❧

HOLD YOUR HORSES PRETTY LITTLE LADY!
Start Here!

Long before you start day one of this book, I started down a path toward emotional healing. And it led me straight into the arms of meditation…and the country. I have tried most forms of meditation and this book combines some of my favorite self-care techniques that I just know you're gonna love!

WELCOME TO YOUR FUN, LITTLE, HANDS-ON MEDIATION KIND-OF RIDE!

FIRST OFF, it's Fun:
While there are some "meaty" stories to spur you on your way, there are also some light and fluffy ones. Not all days are meant for deep contemplation. Sometimes, a reminder to stop and smell the roses is all it takes to slow down and breathe. Other days, you need a good laugh about the fact that no matter how hard you try, you keep killing the roses. The truth is, the longer you practice meditation, the lighter your life will feel. Even the heavy parts.

It's Little:
31 days to be exact. Why so small? Glad you asked. Because I want you to be able to finish the darn thing. Because just like you, I've donated my fair share of huge, unfinished mindfulness journals and meditation books. Enough with the year-long aspirations. Let's just make it through the day. Take your time. Set your own pace. Let these daily meditations flow in and out of your life as you see fit.

Start with Breath:
Each day, you will start with taking three deep, slow, cleansing breaths. Pause your thoughts and focus on your breath as it expands your lungs and abdomen. This will help slow your heart rate and quiet your mind.

Mediation Stories to Read:
Once you've taken your three cleansing breaths, you will read the daily mediation/story. Whether it's about gardening, family, or farm girl kind-of-fun, they will encourage you to find deeper meaning from the mundane and see that beauty is always around.

Self-Reflection Questions/Journal Prompts:
After the daily reading, there will be a few self-reflection questions and a blank lined page where you can write your answers or journal your thoughts. This will help you apply the daily meditation to your own life. And if you're a big-time journaler like me, girl you already know…combine this book with your own journal.

Quotes to Color:
Completing your journal page, you will find a quote to color. Use colored pencils or crayons if you don't want it to bleed through the page. However, feel free to tear the quote out of the book and paint it, color it with markers, hang it on your bathroom mirror, etc.

You can color immediately after the journal page or save it for later. Maybe you could color during the evening as your family watches TV? Not only is coloring relaxing and stress-reducing, but it will also help the message sink in. As you color, you will read and re-read the quote until you know it by heart. Over the next few days, whether driving to work or taking a shower, the quote will seem to float to the top, like a little mantra, reminding you of what matters most in your life.

Songs to Sing:
A few daily meditations refer to a song, either in the story or the quote. I encourage you to download and listen to them. Find a country road and crank it up. Some of the deepest healing and joy is best found through song.

What's the Point?
The point of meditation and this book is to grow inner peace and positive thoughts. This book will not give you a bunch of head knowledge about meditating. This book is in your hands for one main reason: to help you love the life you live. The good. The bad. The ugly. The boring and the beautiful.

So slow down.
Turn off your cell phone.
Take three cleansing breaths.

Kick the kids out and your spouse too. Enough of caring for the rest of the world. This is the place where you get to deeply love the Farm Girl within you.

SADDLE UP SISTER.

We're headed for a good time.

Day 1

DREAM

Taking three deep breaths,
I calm my mind and body.
I welcome this moment just as it is.

Sitting on my front porch swing, ready to have some "me" time, I'd almost always be greeted by a neighbor. I'd smile, chat for a bit, and lose the last precious moments of solitude. Friendly neighbors were not the problem though. If I had to live in a subdivision, thank God I lived in a nice one. And throughout the years I had loved our little suburban home, but my growing love of the land, well…kept growing. Yes, something about this place didn't seem to fit, even though I couldn't see a way out. What about the kids' school, work, friends…we couldn't just leave all that, could we?

Regardless of logic, I decided to write it down. Get it out of my system and move on. So I did. I wrote my dream down on paper: I want to live on land. There, I said it. Enough already. Besides, there's no way it could ever come true anyway. I just knew I couldn't help but dream it.

Then two years later, here we were…moving to the country. In a twist of fate, luck, or maybe the destiny of dreams, my daughter's school was re-zoned. This allowed us to look for homes further out in the country, houses with land. And we found one: a little fixer-upper on five whole acres. Even better, behind us was a 20-acre field. Room to breathe and haybales to count. A dream come true.

I'm not sure what it is about us farm girls that need the farm, but we do. There's a call to the quiet. A need for the nature. An unexplainable love of the land and affection for the animal. We seem to feel better when we're closer to it. And while we can't all pack up and move to the country tomorrow, we can dream.

Yes, we should bloom where we're planted. Right here, right now is always enough. If you can't live on a farm, you can do things to bring the farm to you. Grow a garden, raise baby chicks, shop at the Farmer's Market. But you only have one life. You only have one you. And if your heart belongs on the farm, then dream farm girl, dream. I'm living proof that sometimes, somehow, some way, dreams really do come true.

Write down your dreams, even if they seem too big to come true. Next, write down the dreams that have already come true. Finally, write some things you are thankful for right this very moment.

"In dreams
WE PLANT
the seeds of
OUR FUTURE."

- Unknown

Day 2

TROPHY

Taking three deep breaths,
I calm my mind and body.
I welcome this moment just as it is.
It is enough, just as I am enough.

I'm a morning journaler and coffee drinker…at least on my less hurried mornings. Cross-legged on the couch or on my front porch are my go-to spots. And my go-to companions? Poppy and Pumpkin, our country cat and precious pup. They often compete for my lap and take turns sharing the trophy. This morning, however, Pumpkin not only was snuggled beside my lap, she had jumped in it, curling herself in a cat-like ball. Petting her, I remembered how far she'd come to even be able to do this. Like many of us, she had endured trauma and suffering early in her life.

Pumpkin was not born into a life of privilege or even love. Shaking, afraid, and hiding behind the tire of a car, she was found abandoned in a parking lot. After searching for her owner, she was finally placed for adoption when they could not find anyone to claim her. A three-month-old, tan and white, Papillion-dachshund mix, with big butterfly-like ears had not even been missed.

After adoption, we noticed she would cower and sometimes even shake in fear when we'd pet her. Instead of curling up next to us on the couch, she'd hop down and curl up next to the fireplace. While we watched television, she'd watch us. Riding in the car, I'd hold her in my lap to let her see outside. But instead of hanging her head out the window like most other car-riding dogs, she'd bury her face in my arms and shake vigorously.

She could have easily worn that collar of shame for the rest of her life: "Parking Lot Pumpkin." But thankfully, those days seem long forgotten. She seems to have died to the past. Living only here, in the present moment, jumping in my lap, to win her trophy.

While it is true that we can learn from our past, it is more true that the past is no place to live. Hands may have hurt, but not all will. Some may have forgotten, but another will remember, and the world is too big, bright, and beautiful not to hang your head out the window to adore. New life is happening. It is happening now. May we jump in its lap and win our trophy.

Are you stuck somewhere in the past, retelling a story over and over in your head? Write one or more reasons you are thankful now. What "new life" is happening in your life? Focus your full attention on the gifts of this present moment.

"DIE TO THE PAST EVERY MOMENT.

You don't need it."

- Eckhart Tolle

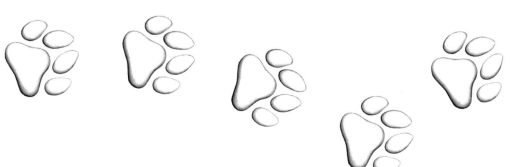

Day 3
FLOAT

Taking three deep breaths,
I calm my mind and body.
I welcome this moment just as it is.
It is enough, just as I am enough.

Meditation carries you deeper, helps you see and know the ground called stable, the mind called peace. It's an intentional path to go beyond little man-made thoughts. A willingness to see past the roles you play. Past your gender and race. A desire to dip into the realm of knowing. Shedding the world of form and connecting more deeply with your true self: Being.

Yet, this world of form seems to keep me stuck in the mind. Thoughts, labels, and judgements seem to rule the emotions, rule the day. And at times, I seem helpless to their torment. Think this. Label that. Curse the bloody traffic. And even more than the little problems, are the never-ending list of "real problems." Bills, work, relationships, the messy house, the dinner, the groceries, and the list goes on and on and on. And my mind, right along with it.

Yet, sitting still, seeking a world that stops, I can see clearer through the clouds. Though I have paused, they have not. Slowly, they roll on. On and on, like an endless list of clouds.

Are not my thoughts, my "problems," the same? Right when one is gone, isn't there another one right behind? Why do I go along with them? Even now, my mind is telling me, "Get up and get going! This cloud watching is silly. This meditation, pointless. What does it really do anyway?" Yet, I've done enough doing to know it doesn't do one bloody thing. It leaves me worn out, wiped out, and weary.

No, today I'm doing rest. I'm doing meditation. Because I've learned the hard way, life doesn't have to be hard. Life isn't hard. It's my thoughts that make it so.

But I'm not my thoughts.
I'm more than mind.
More than matter.
I'm rising above all that noise.
And today, I'm floating on a cloud.

Practice becoming aware of your thoughts, rather than being held captive by them. Don't judge or criticize, but simply notice them. Often, our thoughts can be formed from too much past, future, or fear within us. In the light of your presence, their grip will lessen. Let them come, see them, and lovingly, let them go. Rest in who you are, not in what the mind says.

"DON'T LET your mind BULLY your body."

— Unknown

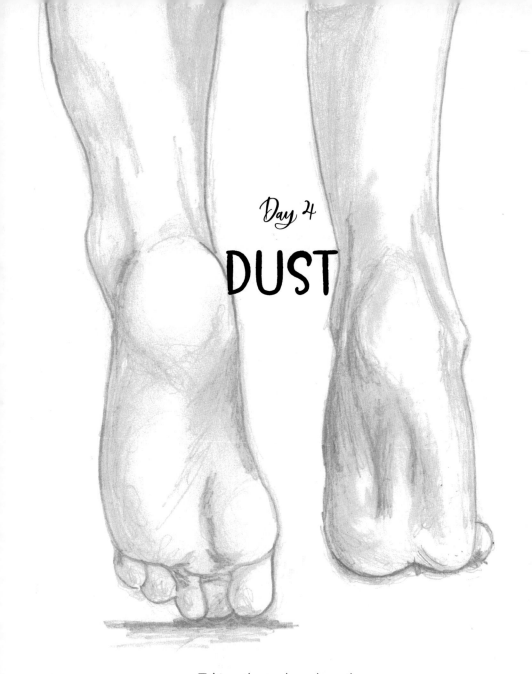

Day 4

DUST

Taking three deep breaths,
I calm my mind and body.
I welcome this moment just as it is.
It is enough, just as I am enough.

I consider myself a backyard gardener and enjoy trying all sorts of methods. One year, I decided to try deep-mulch gardening. I was so excited because this garden was going to be huge. An in-ground, bigger than big garden. I sprouted seeds indoors and even tested the soil. But I forgot about the most important part: it hurts to walk barefoot on wood chips.

As a child, I grew up in a time without cell phones or computers. I rode my bike till after dark and ran around barefoot. I grew up in the South, so it was warm enough to warrant the freedom. I carried this barefoot freedom into adulthood and likewise into my garden. But now, I had created a football field of wood chips that I couldn't even walk on. I laughed it off but decided future gardens would have to be suitable for bare feet. Why? Because my feet were not just created to walk on the Earth, but rather to be a part of it.

Somewhere between the cave and the castle, we seem to have evolved ourselves right out of nature…right out of ourselves. How quickly we forget the very dust from which we were formed. Fear may have told us it's safer to wear shoes, but it shouldn't tell us it's unsafe to go barefoot. It is through our bare feet that the soil can ground us once more, allowing a sense of calm and clarity to return.

This Earth is not just here to be observed. It's here to be experienced, felt…to be loved. So today, even as a "grown-up," go outside, take your shoes off, and silently shout a Braveheart "Freedom" as you run barefoot in your own backyard. Being one with nature once more. One with the you, you really are.

Grass to toe.
Wind to hair.
Dust…to dust.

Many people report an improvement in chronic stress, pain, anxiety, or depression after trying grounding therapy. Simply walk barefoot in the grass, sand, or even mud. You can also take a picnic and lie on the ground. Give it a try and write how you felt or what you experienced.

"For you are DUST and to DUST you shall return" Genesis 3:19, ESV

Day 5

ADVENTURE

Taking three deep breaths,
I calm my mind and body.
I welcome this moment just as it is.
It is enough, just as I am enough.

Three weeks of living in our little fixer upper and I was thankful the bathtub worked. Renovating a house in the country was no small chore. I was fresh out of the bath, blind as a bat without my glasses on, when I thought I saw my dog, Pumpkin. Her little black nose seemed to be peaking around the corner of the door. I called her to come, but she disappeared. I yelled down the hall to my husband, Brad, "Is Pumpkin out there with you?" "Yeah, she's right here. Why?" he answered. Screams from the bathroom could be heard as I yelled, "Oh my word! I think I just called a mouse to come to me!"

Jumping to his feet like Elmer Fudd and shouting to Pumpkin like she was his hunting dog, I heard Brad say, "Let's go get that mouse Pumpkin!" All I could think was, what? No! Do not use my precious, pristine Pumpkin as a mouse hunter! Yet, seconds later, here we were: Pumpkin, chasing the mouse from under the bed; my husband, holding a broom, cheering her on; and me, with dripping wet hair in tears, blocking the door with boxes. Good lord, how had this become my life? I felt like I was living in a nightmare, witnessing a murder. All of sudden I heard Brad yell, "Drop it, Pumpkin, drop it." Then whack, down came the broom, as I sobbed, "I cannot do this! I did not move here for this!" Soon after, Brad and Pumpkin came strutting down the hall like they had killed the fatted calf.

Had those two blind eyes been more like crystal balls, I'm not sure I would have moved here. But we didn't move to the country just for the quiet; we also moved for the adventure. I mean, what's the fun if you already know the way? There are mountains to climb and mice to be hunted. Challenges that help you grow and others to help you bend. Why read the story if you already know the end?

Thankfully, that was the first and last indoor mouse we had and the hunting team of three disbanded when our stray cat, Poppy, showed up. It was as if my cries had been heard from Heaven and a cat was sent to save me. Thank. You. God. As for these two blind eyes, well, it turns out they give just enough sight. Just enough for me to have learned, I better laugh a lot and hang on tight.

What are some of your favorite adventures? What did you learn from them? How can adventures help you grow, learn to laugh, or let go? What are some new adventures you would like to plan? They can be big, like moving homes or just for fun, like learning a new skill or trying a new hobby.

_____

_____

_____

_____

_____

_____

_____

_____

_____

_____

_____

_____

_____

_____

_____

_____

_____

_____

_____

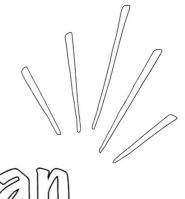

"Life is an
ADVENTURE
ENJOY
the ride"
—Unknown

Day 6

STAPLE

Taking three deep breaths,
I calm my mind and body.
I welcome this moment just as it is.
It is enough, just as I am enough.

Some things are staples of the South. Like front porch sittin' and sweet tea. Or biscuits with gravy. Some things seem rooted in our past, yet ever near us in our present. And though while young, I never cared too much for sittin' or front porches; as I grow, they have both had a way of growing on me. Maybe it's because the duties of motherhood leave feet that ache. Or chores and cleaning the house leaves me with a back that breaks. Or maybe it's because I'm Southern through and through and these old bones know when it's time to sit for a spell. Whatever the reason, the front porch seems to call my name like the wind called to Pocahontas and happily, I return to her.

Now, I've become quite the front porch connoisseur over the years. Decorating for this season or that. A throw pillow here, a wreath there. A succulent for this table or a potted plant for that spot. A comfortable chair, even a little love seat and ottoman grace my presence as it calls me to come and sip my warm cup of coffee. And even though I can't use it year-round due to the sweltering summer months, it's become a staple of my sanity.

There's no denying it, there is just something therapeutic about the front porch. Whether you've got sweet tea or water, coffee, or soda. Whether you've got time to sit or you don't. There's a reason to make time for this outdoor therapy and maybe now more than ever. Our overworked lives leave little room to sit and sip or wave at a neighbor driving by. I agree, life spins fast and busy. But I also agree it's high time to pump the breaks.

There's more to life than work and consuming or bills and chores. The honest truth is, we spin so fast we spin right past the point. It's when we rest that we can once again remember and know all we love and hold dear. So, if it's been a while since you've sat for a spell, head on out and see for yourself. Gaze upon a bird, a cloud, or some trees. I think you'll come to know, like me, your front porch is a much-needed staple.

What are some ways you could spruce up your front porch to enjoy it more? Is there a rocking chair you'd like to add or maybe even a front porch swing? Take time to "nest" your area of rest. Show honor to the space that can breathe new life into your bones. Consider inviting a neighbor over to join you one afternoon. Brew some tea and consider the time well wasted!

"The Porch:

Where wasting time is considered time well wasted."

– Unknown

Day 7
WILDFLOWERS

Taking three deep breaths,
I calm my mind and body.
I welcome this moment just as it is.
It is enough, just as I am enough.

I guess it shouldn't come as a surprise that I found flowers healing during a season of grief. There is reason they show up at hospitals and funerals. Long before I figured it out, people have known that when you don't know what to say or do, send flowers. They seem to speak a type of love that is lost on our human language. Just looking at them seems to connect us to a different realm not made of dust and bone, grass or sky.

But my dad didn't have a traditional funeral or burial. He was cremated and we remembered him with a small home memorial service. People gathered and shared a meal, but I didn't leave with my arms full of flowers. I didn't think a thing about it until a couple months later when I was out walking my dog. Spring was in bloom and so were the wildflowers. As I walked, I began to notice them and before I knew it, had gathered a full bouquet.

I was estranged from my dad for 17 years. I had only reconnected with him three years before his passing and as it turned out, I was the one to find him deceased in his apartment. His breathing machine had broken, and he died in his sleep without it. He had lived with back surgeries and pain, as well as failing physical and mental health for years. I had feared this day long before it arrived, yet nothing could prepare me. After crying off and on for two weeks, my body went into "business mode." As the executor of my dad's estate, I didn't have time to process. I didn't want to process. I felt I had tried to "save" my dad off and on my entire childhood and now, here I was, all grown up, and still…couldn't save him. It was all too much, and I just wanted to move on.

Coming back to the house, I brought the flowers to my face, letting the petals kiss my cheeks so I could smell them but instead, I heard them "speak" as this thought instantly came to mind: "I love you in millions of ways, rainbows of ways. I will love you in millions more." Silent tears began to fall as my hardened outer shell began to soften once again. I didn't know if Dad, my Creator, or the flowers themselves had sent that message, but I didn't care.

In that moment, I knew I was being loved, being held. The tears I was holding as hostages broke free, as I lowered my weapons. I was defenseless against this quiet voice of love, loving me through the flowers. It felt as if the wildflowers were re-wilding me too, and I thanked God for it.

I've never been "all business" and never should be. I'm not suited for an office or a lack of emotions or tears. When I feel, it's best if the world and my heart just lets me get it out. The wildflowers seemed to know this better than I. It's as if they could sense my pain as I walked by them and knew I needed a hug that only they could give.

That spring, I planted my first patch of wildflowers and have done so every year since then. I know now the silent language they speak. The comfort they alone can give when there is nothing anyone can say or do. And even though I don't hear them speak often, I know they are there when I need them to re-wild me once again. Untame me from business mode or gently hold me as I breathe them in. They love me from another realm. One not made of human or house, death or disease. It's eternal and timeless, filled with millions of rainbows made of love.

Thank goodness, not all seasons are filled with grief. But flowers make life better, no matter the reason. So next time, don't race right past the flowers in the store or even glance over the ones outside your door. Take a wildflower walk or grow some of your own. Let the petals kiss your cheeks and feel their healing power. If there's one thing I know farm girl, it's that you and I belong among the wildflowers.

*Download and listen to the song *Wildflowers* by Tom Petty

"You belong among the wildflowers"

– Tom Petty

Day 8

MUD

Taking three deep breaths,
I calm my mind and body.
I welcome this moment just as it is.
It is enough, just as I am enough.

Try as they might, the pig's water bowl would not stay put. They'd fill it up and she'd knock it over: Emma, that is. The big pig featured in the documentary, *The Biggest Little Farm*. If you've not seen it, you must! You will love it. And quickly, love Emma the pig too. But more than wanting water, Emma wanted mud. More than the functional uses of her bowl, she saw it fit for play.

For the most part, pigs wallow in mud to keep cool, remove pesky parasites, or because their DNA hardwires them to do so. But it's also comforting. And as Emma proves, if the mud is missing, the water bowl will do the trick. She teaches us that life's not worth living without the mud.

And the same can be said for humans, although I doubt most of us would choose mud over water. But we should choose something in addition to the necessities of life. Unfortunately, we see play as trivial instead of the oxygen it is. But it holds great value. Far greater than we see.

When we play, it's not just that we give our overworked selves a break. It's that our furrowed brow softens. The mouth smiles. Tight shoulders fall and even that chattering mind can pause. How much power a simple crayon holds. How much your music time really does matter. Yes, sometimes, it is the sewing that saves us or the hike that heals.

Playing is not something you outgrow just because you grew up. It fits you like a glove every time you put it on. Sometimes, we just forget and need a pig's-eye view. Because there's more to life than water. Much more.

There's mud.

Do you make time for playing? What would feel fun to do? Color, paint, write, play an instrument, garden, learn to sew, or bake? Is there someone you could invite to play with you? Write down some ways you want to play and commit to a specific day and time until it becomes more habitual. Notice how you feel before and after your "playtime".

"Life is like a box of crayons."

— John Mayer

Day 9

WISH

Taking three deep breaths,
I calm my mind and body.
I welcome this moment just as it is.
It is enough, just as I am enough.

When I close my eyes, I can see it plain as day. Chickens in the yard, the horse by the fence, a sheep baaa-ing in the background, and my hair flowing in long, golden locks. I AM Princess Buttercup from the movie, *The Princess Bride*. And my husband is Westley, the handsome farmhand. All I need is to whisper, "Farm boy!" and my Westley will come running. I can see it now, "Farm boy! Fetch me some eggs." "Farm boy! Milk the cow." And what is my beloved's response? "As you wish."

Yet, reality is far from fantasy. First off, my hair is flowing locks of frizz, not golden strands of gorgeous. We have no cow to milk or horse to ride. My "Westley" works on the ole handy dandy computer, not tractor. And even though he works hard to make my every dream come true, rarely, if ever, has his response been, "As you wish."

While a farm girl can dream, the truth is, I'm a non-fiction lover first. Romance can always be found in reality. Marriages may not be made of sunshine and rainbows, but they are sown in seeds of love. Seeds that sprout today and bloom tomorrow. Seeds that survive the storm and weather the wind.

In reality, the Dad from *A Christmas Story*, weaving a tapestry of muttered, unknown curse words while working on the house, comes to mind. Or even Steve Martin's character from *Father of the Bride*, as he rips open the hot dog bun package. These are the occasional, yet honest and endearing images of my farm boy. He may not be perfect, but he is perfect for me. To me, he's even more handsome than Westley. He's also extremely handy and even domestic. He can fix anything and often cooks dinner and does the laundry. Maybe I am Princess Buttercup after all? Maybe my farm boy is just as I wished.

Yes, when I close my eyes, it's clear to see. He's even more.

He's just what I need.

Today, reflect on the one you love. Think of the love between you. The ways you both show you care. Write down all the things you love about them and are thankful for them. Look through old photos and choose one to print. Let it be a reminder that you are both just what you need and never doubt again.

"I'll never doubt again."

— Princess Buttercup

Day 10

GOOD MORNING

Taking three deep breaths,
I calm my mind and body.
I welcome this moment just as it is.
It is enough, just as I am enough.

I, like most Americans, have little ample time in the mornings. Getting my daughter to school, making breakfast, packing lunch, brewing the coffee, feeding the dog, and not to mention the cat, all seem to rush the morning right out the window. Running through the drive through, making ends meet, picking up dinner because you're too exhausted to cook or clean. I mean, it's just our American way. Sure, we can all appreciate a good sunrise, but who's got time to soak up the rays on any given American day?

But regardless of the rush, there's something sweet about the mornings. Maybe it's because the rest of my family is still asleep, and the house is quiet. Or maybe it's because the sunrise peaks its head just over the top of our massive barn roof. Or maybe it's because the sun itself seems to be greeting me, in a little good morning kiss. Whatever the multitude of reasons, I have fallen head-over-heels in love with the morning. And if I wake up early enough, I can even squeeze in a cup of coffee and journaling…my favorite!

Not everyone is a journaler and that's okay. I wasn't always either. But there's something about a pen and paper. The way it helps me listen to my very own voice within. The brain dump that seems to loosen the ole creative juices or emotionally ground me once again. I even journal my conversations with God and for me, it's been lifesaving. Somehow, some way, this old pen and paper seem to be doing more than simply passing the time. It seems to be writing the story of my life, the very nature of who I am.

It's true, there's joy to be found in a silent, sleeping house. A set appointment made for just you and the morning. Wake up early. Watch the sunrise as you sip the warmth from your cup. Grab a journal and a pen and put your feet up. Let the hurry be hushed. Let the worry be calmed. Yes, we're Americans, but first and foremost, we're farm girls, and we've got more important things to do than run out the door or make the beds. There is silence to be heard and journals to be written and even a sunrise kiss to greet us upon our heads.

What do you love most about the mornings? If you are too busy of a weekday, give yourself a quiet morning on a weekend. Buy a new journal and fill the pages. Sit somewhere you can feel the morning sun and be warmed to your core.

"Good morning morning Sunshine"

– Unknown

Day 11

SMILE

Taking three deep breaths,
I calm my mind and body.
I welcome this moment just as it is.
It is enough, just as I am enough.

For quite some time I have recycled. I know the need to reduce, reuse, and recycle plastics, paper, aluminum, and glass. What I didn't know was how harmful food waste is to our landfills. It releases methane gas that increases global warming. From podcasts like *The Joe Gardener Show* to documentaries such as *A Life On Our Planet*, my knowledge of how humans affect the world grew. And what I learned was not only shocking but also life changing.

No longer did I just see plastic and paper towels as the only problem, but now understood how food waste was damaging too. So, I decided to do my part and compost. I had the normal concerns about critters getting in and what type of bin to use but decided to start with a simple pile. For every bucket of food scraps, I'd add some wood chips on top. No air, no water, no turning it once a week. Just food waste with wood chips. Of course, if I turned and watered the pile, I'd have black gold for the garden, but I try to keep things easy. If it's too tedious or time-consuming, especially in the beginning, I know I'd quit.

As you can guess, it wasn't ready for my garden come spring, or even fall, but what I did end up having was compost magic. In a matter of months, my compost was sprouting all sorts of plants but most of all pumpkins. I even transplanted some to my garden, but others I left growing in the pile. By fall, the compost had produced a cluster of miniature white pumpkins grown without any tending to or care. I couldn't believe it!

I'd like to tell you that by now I'm a composting master, but the truth is I'm far from it. I still don't turn it often or water it. It may take five years to get that precious black gold, but for now, just reducing the methane gas makes me feel better. Besides, I'm sure from time to time, seeds will sprout on their own, right from the pile. And when your compost grows a pumpkin while at the same time reducing global warming, well, there's no better reason to smile.

In what ways do you reduce, reuse, or recycle? Do you want to learn more through podcasts or shows? A great TV show to try is Growing A Greener World (available on PBS or YouTube). Have you tried composting? Write down some ways you want to take better care of the Earth or reduce waste. If we all take one small step, it will result in one huge step forward.

"We do not inherit the land from our ancestors, we borrow it from our children."

– Native American Proverb

SISTERS

Taking three deep breaths,
I calm my mind and body.
I welcome this moment just as it is.
It is enough, just as I am enough.

I don't think we would have met without our dogs. It was like a scene from the movie, 101 Dalmatians. The humans minding their own business and the dogs not minding a bit. We were the only two people who brought our dogs to the church softball game. They were supposed to keep us company, but before we knew it leashes were tangled, tails were wagging, and unbeknownst to me, I was meeting my future best friend, Haley. A few weeks later, I gave her a call her and we hung up friends.

Since then, we've had babies and marriages, moved homes and changed jobs. We've talked too many hours to count and taken a girls' trip every year. We've climbed mountains, tried our best to tent camp, and gotten lost in the woods. We can laugh till we cry or cry till we laugh. Through the ups and the downs, we've shared it all. So much so, that by now, all these years later (seventeen to be exact), she's more than a friend, she's my sister.

There are some friends who come to visit and others who come to stay, but then some who seem to be made from your own DNA. I'll never forget a retreat Haley and I went on. It was supposed to be a silent retreat, and how we got ourselves into this one is beyond me. Somehow, we were supposed to go an entire weekend without talking. Thankfully, Haley is creative, and she communicated just fine through her face, huge eyes, or body language. The purpose of the retreat was to grow spiritually through the silence, but really it just improved our sign language skills. Yes, it seems we were in fact cut from the same giggling cloth.

We laugh at all our Lucille and Ethel moments and say we're making memories for the nursing home, but I know it's more than that. All us "sister-friends" do, because sisters don't just hold hands, they hold hearts. They go on adventures and make us brave. They help us laugh and keep us sane. And deep down, we know we have ESP. The truth is, somewhere along the way, you become part of each other. So, whether in this life or the next, may we never forget and always remember the love of a farm girl sister.

Take a moment of silence to think of your farm girl sisters. Use the space below to write why you are thankful for them or some of your favorite memories. Consider taking a photo of what you write and sharing it with them.

"When we're old, let's move in together and pretend we're the Golden Girls"

– Unknown

Day 13

FOLLOW

Taking three deep breaths,
I calm my mind and body.
I welcome this moment just as it is.
It is enough, just as I am enough.

I wanted to grow flowers but the space I had just wouldn't do. Three raised beds was not enough. So we added another and this one was for flowers only. No carrots, no squash, no tomato could crowd this precious soil. And while not all sprouted, what did grow grew like weeds. I had Zinnias and Mexican Sunflowers for days, no…months.

At some point though, the flowers began to have visitors. A butterfly here, a butterfly there. One would land and then another fly away. Sometimes even two would share a bloom. Eventually, it dawned on me, I hadn't just grown flowers, I grew a wildlife habitat! The thought came like a lightning bolt: "Get your camera girl!" Yes! Of course, let's capture this beauty up close.

By now, I not only had a butterfly sanctuary, but a bumble bee and hummingbird haven too. And occasionally, they would even land on me. I was zoomed in, laser-focused, losing track of time, and deep into my kind of heaven. From then on, I cut fewer and fewer flowers. Feeding my new friends and capturing them on camera became my new-found love.

Although I was in my own backyard, I had no clue where this little flowerbed was taking me. At first, filling an empty vase was my only hope. But in the end, I realized they had filled much more. Not only was I a backyard flower gardener, but now, I was also a backyard nature photographer!

I'll be honest; half the time I have no clue what I'm doing or where I'm going. I've just learned to stop caring. Life seems to be carrying me anyway. Right when I think I want to grow flowers, life shows me there's so much more. So I give up. Who cares. Life's too fun, too big and adventurous to tame. So I won't. I'll let life be wild and remember that I'm right where I need to be. The truth is, when I follow what I love, I will always find a little bit more of me.

Outside of work or paid passions, write down at least three things you love to do or would love to try. Out of the three, which one would you like to do the most? Choose a specific day and time this week you could make this happen. How would it feel to bring more of this activity into your life?

_____

_____

_____

_____

_____

_____

_____

_____

_____

_____

_____

_____

_____

_____

_____

_____

_____

_____

_____

"Follow WHAT YOU Love."

— Holly Love King

Day 14

SHOOT THE MOON

Taking three deep breaths,
I calm my mind and body.
I welcome this moment just as it is.
It is enough, just as I am enough.

The lockdown of 2020 during the COVID-19 pandemic left us stir- crazy like everyone else. We watched and re-watched movies. Popped popcorn, baked bread, and cooked up comfort food like we were professional chefs. My daughter and I learned how to embroider. My husband and stepson fixed up a go-cart and put it to use. We were thankful for our wide-open spaces and our little house in the country. Our home was a haven of comfort for sure, but after awhile, nothing could prevent us from feeling cooped up.

Well, that was until we discovered Rook. One night after exhausting all other board games, my husband, Brad, asked if we wanted to learn a new game. We jumped at the idea and Brad's eyes lit up. He had grown up playing with his grandfather and couldn't wait to teach us. As Brad began teaching, all I could think was, this game had to be invented before television or electricity. It had so many little rules for this and rules for that, I felt lost. And that's when he lowered the boom on us. We had to play in teams of two, diagonal from each other. And what would you know...our "assigned" dinner table seats landed me and my 10-year-old stepson, Braden, as partners.

Our eyes met wide as saucers, whispering, "Do you understand how to play?" or "Have you been paying attention?" It was obvious we were both clueless. Neither of us are known for our game night wins. A few rounds in, with Brad telling us which cards to play, he began to tell us about more advanced moves. Advanced? Braden and I were bumbling on the beginner level! Don't confuse us even more. Brad continued, "Eventually, you'll learn how to 'Shoot the Moon.'" Shoot the moon? More like shoot your eye out buddy, if you tell me one more rule.

No surprise, Braden and I lost. But we laughed the entire way toward our defeat. Over the next few weeks, we continued to play, change partners, and I continued to lose. Heaven help me, I may never learn how to shoot the moon, but one thing I hope is for game nights with my family to come often and soon.

Plan a game night with family, friends, or one of each. Think of ways to make it creative. Have a themed game night, play only classics, or buy a new game and make finger foods. Write down fun memories of past game nights. Promise yourself you'll make new memories and shoot the moon soon!

"A FAMILY that PLAYS together STAYS TOGETHER."

– Unknown

Day 15

PEACE

Taking three deep breaths,
I calm my mind and body.
I welcome this moment just as it is.
It is enough, just as I am enough.

Far too often, my mind seeks a plan or a solution. It seems I'd prefer to be a fortune teller rather than a farm girl. I want to know the weather tomorrow, what's for dinner, and how's the ole retirement fund performing? An insurance policy for this, a nest egg for that, what if we lose our jobs, or God-forbid get cancer? Questions swirl about in this ole brain, like I'm Dorothy standing before the great Wizard of Oz, but no prediction is ever given. I'm left standing with my list of questions and silence as my only answer. It's enough to drive a figure-it-out-kinda-girl mad! Or at least just to the point of insanity, well, maybe almost insanity.

But what's insane is doing the same thing over and over expecting different results. And though I'm a slow learner, I can say one thing has begun to sink in during my forty-plus years…we can't know the future. And as much as I try, I can't change it, fix it, solve it, glue it, tape it, or even shape it exactly as I demand. I can't change people and I can't change the past. Heck, it's about near impossible to change myself. It's beyond obvious, this life is not about predictability or control.

Yet, when I quiet my mind and take those three cleansing breaths, I see far past those noisy little thoughts. All those questions demanding an answer. They all seem to hush, at least for a moment, as I show back up and remind them who's in charge. It's me. The true me, the one living at my core. The one who doesn't need a wizard named Oz or a Google chrome bar. I don't need the weather or even the stock market to perform as I desire. All I need, I somehow seem to already have…peace. A peace that passes all understanding. A peace that grounds me, even though my ground is still shaking. A peace that warms me, even though I'm cold and a peace that holds me even though I'm alone.

Yes, when I pause, it's clear to see…

Farm girl, you already have all you ever need.

Take three cleansing breaths, quiet your mind, and pause your thoughts. What do you see right now? Write the things you are thankful for. Let the peace of this present moment remind you that you already have all you ever need.

"Farm girl you already have ALL you ever need."

– Holly Love King

Day 16

COUNTRY ROADS

Taking three deep breaths,
I calm my mind and body.
I welcome this moment just as it is.
It is enough, just as I am enough.

Still trying to convince my city-girl daughter, Scout, that moving to the country was not a mistake as we headed out the door for her first day of sixth grade. I figured our new school commute would be filled with dreamy picturesque mornings watching the sunrise or counting cows. On this country, two-lane highway it was just you and the Tennessee land. Big blue skies, white fluffy clouds, and red barns to boot.

Boy was I wrong. That first morning we didn't notice the cows or the sunshine. Instead, all we could see was the roadkill. Telling each other to "Look away," or asking each other, "What was that?" was about all we discussed. When we hit the parking lot our eyes were as big as saucers and I tried to convince Scout this was surely a one-time occurrence.

But by the time seventh grade rolled around, we were roadkill experts. Instead of shock and awe, we rarely if ever even commented on the dearly departed, except for one day that neither of us will soon forget. Not only did we sail right past a dead skunk, possum, raccoon, and armadillo, but also a beautiful red fox, and that about brought us to tears. We had barely recovered from the fox when out of nowhere the fattest little brown field mouse ran right across the road. I didn't say a word, praying to God that Scout had been looking the other way. Soon she said, "MOM! Did you just see that? Was that a mouse?!" Trying to be convincing I answered straight-faced and serious, "No, honey, I'm sure it was just a squirrel." "A squirrel? Mom! You're lying! You know that was a mouse!"

We both began laughing as I had to admit, yes, good lord, it was a mouse! Heaven help me, I felt like Noah driving the ark and the flood was a-comin'. These country critters seemed bound and determined to flock to me like their leader. All I could think was, "Are you kidding me? I'm trying to help my daughter love the country, not want to leave it!" I was certain that once grown, my city-girl Scout, would never want to drive this country road home.

Thankfully, there's more to a country road than the roadkill. I learned this best when I was in college. A small university in the middle of nowhere West Tennessee. Even though I'm a Nashville-native and everyone envisions it as rolling hills and pastures, the suburbs are still filled with houses, not horses. The city filled with skyscrapers. The streets with strip malls. You have to drive a ways out to find the open road.

But two months before my freshman year in college, I had placed my beautiful baby boy, Andrew, for open adoption. It was a private Christian college, not known for their fondness of the out-of-wedlock, pregnant teenage girl. And even though I did my best to hide that fact, the truth was, my heart was breaking. Grieving mixed with growing and trying not to become the next "failure to launch" was all a bit much. Some days it felt as if those college kids and walls were crumbling right on top of me and I was suffocating. The only way I could breathe was to get in my car and get the hell out of that place. Drive and not stop driving. Let myself cry and not stop crying.

Those big, open roads seemed big enough to hold my grief and my heart. They were empty. No cars. No people. No judgement. They just let me be. Little by little I began to learn the quiet country road was my new comfort zone. I don't think I would have survived those years without them. It was just one of many "country seeds" planted within me that now, all these years later, had me trying to plant one within my own daughter.

I know that Scout may choose to live near a skyscraper instead of a stable. She may never garden or compost and lord knows, she'll never love passing roadkill. But life has a way of forcing us to grow up. Giving us things we can handle and things we can't. Things to hold onto and others to let go of. For Scout and all of us, it usually just takes a bit of living before we have the wisdom to know, that all country roads take you home.

*Download and listen to the song *Take Me Home, Country Roads* by John Denver

"Country ROADS take me HOME."

– John Denver

Day 17

CHERRIES

Taking three deep breaths,
I calm my mind and body.
I welcome this moment just as it is.
It is enough, just as I am enough.

I don't know what it is about us gardeners, but we seem to all have the same problem: eyes bigger than our stomachs. Even seasoned gardeners tend to over grow. Bowls aren't just filled, they're stuffed full. It seems we find just as much joy in giving produce away as we do in growing it. Each year, I plan and map out the plot doing my best to stay calm. Some years, I even swear I'm not going to garden, because I tend to make such a mess of things. Yet spring after spring, the bug bites and before I know it, I'm knee-deep in the dirt with my husband hollering from the house, "I told ya so."

And like all vegetable growers, I agree, you can't have a garden without tomatoes. Unfortunately though, in my house I'm the main tomato connoisseur. And while I can give those things away like hot cakes, I'm quickly up to my eyeballs in tomatoes. Of course, my future goal is to preserve them, but for my younger years, the main goal has been preserving my own sanity.

So much so that by now, the poor things often have to tend and fend for themselves. By the dog days of summer, I'm dog-gone done too. And this previous year took the cake. Neglect, drought, or too much rain left my tomatoes green and dwarfed. About ten tomato plants, and only one seemed to be thriving in my absence: the cherries!

Ahh, the blessed cherries. Just as one cluster was harvested, the next would be ripening. There's nothing sweeter than running from the kitchen to your garden grocery store half-way though dinner prep. You feel like a pioneer, homesteading rock star. "Oh, we need cherry tomatoes? Please, by all means, let me go fetch some."

I've come to accept that not all of my garden will grow. I do what I can and have fun while I learn. All us gardeners can relate. You don't get good overnight and you can't grow without rain and the bees. It's true, our eyes may always be bigger than our stomachs, but one thing I hope for you, and for me…may our bowls be ever so full of the blessed cherries.

What is something you like to grow or would like to learn how to grow? Many people say they feel better after playing in the dirt through gardening, whether it's a simple flowerbed or a few potted plants. You can even try growing herbs indoors. Write down future growing plans and dream big! Trust me, dirty fingernails are a farm girls' therapy.

"LIFE'S A bowl of cherry tomatoes."

- Holly Love King

Day 18

LOVE

Taking three deep breaths,
I calm my mind and body.
I welcome this moment just as it is.
It is enough, just as I am enough.

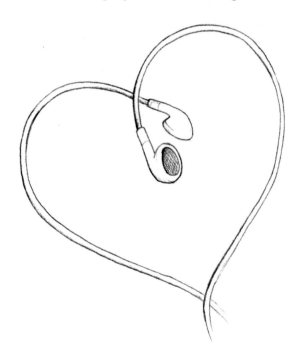

A nursery, fit for a barnyard dance, welcomed our precious daughter, Scout. Green paint, a chicken, cow, and a pig decorated her walls. It's not that I was trying to turn her into a cowgirl. I was just sharing what I loved. And as a toddler, I continued. I'd take Scout outdoors most every day. In her sandbox, I'd even bury plastic toy insects for her to find and identify. I wanted her up close and unafraid of nature, just like me. And for a while, it worked.

But somewhere around the age of two or three, Scout became obsessed with nail polish. Fine, I thought. Let's do nails. Once a week? Okay, no problem. Then, once a day? Well, that seemed a bit tedious. Then, demanding she paint them all by herself? Well, now that just seemed ridiculous. She was two! And what about our nature walks? Bug collecting? Or mud pies? No, those seemed to be quickly replaced for the love of everything girl. Make-up, nails, and dress-up for days. We quickly became best friends with the nail polish aisle, and don't even get me started on when she discovered press-on nails. Once, at the age of seven, she even talked her naïve stepdad into buying her leopard print nails and wore them to second grade! Our baby girl looked like the next wanna be Kardashian.

And while trying to tame the diva, something has happened along the way. I've learned life's much more fun living with different than living with the same. Don't get me wrong; I can fantasize about a child that likes to hike or a kid that's not afraid of bees. But that's not my girl and therefore, not the one for me. It seems our Creator knows we don't need mirrors to help us see.

We need love to come in and through us all. Love to be the brick that breaks down our wall. I don't need a carbon copy of myself. I don't need more of the same. The truth is, thanks to Scout, I love pedicures and I've learned it's fun to change. There's more to life than gardening and bare feet. There's a world full of different. A world full and free. A world that's calling…to you and to me. Love one another, great and small. For love is the answer, after all.

Who or what in your life has helped you grow past your comfort zones? How could non-judgment or non-resistance help you connect to those close to you? If you struggle to accept others who seem different, let Dolly help! Download the song, *Why,* by Dolly Parton & Mavis Staples. Then, Crank. It. Up.

_____

_____

_____

_____

_____

_____

_____

_____

_____

_____

_____

_____

_____

_____

_____

_____

_____

_____

"Let Everyone be ALL that they wanna be."

– Dolly Parton

HIGH COTTON

Taking three deep breaths,
I calm my mind and body.
I welcome this moment just as it is.
It is enough, just as I am enough.

There's a famous prayer that says, "Give us this day our daily bread," but I like at least a month's worth of bread in my pantry. I like to know we have what we need and then some, even if we can't eat it all before it goes bad. It's not that I want to be wasteful, I just want to be sure we don't run out. But there's a simpler way of life, one that focuses on the day at hand, that I need to once again see.

It's not just the abundance of bread I seem to hoard but closets full of clothes or craft supplies too. From storage bins of stuff to attics full of antiques, I swear I could open up my own thrift shop. Somehow, despite my best efforts to purge and clean out, there's always more to give away. But I want to live a simple life. Have more with less. Yes, it's fun to collect shoes and dresses, gardening tools and kitchen gadgets, but enough already. How much more do I need?

Our culture shouts the message loud and clear, "Consume, consume, and please consume just a bit little more." Every year the magazines and malls convince me it's out with the old and in the with new and blindly I follow right along. New clothes, new make-up, new furniture and décor. But don't I have enough stuff already? No, I don't want my house to look outdated or my wardrobe either, but how often do I need a makeover? At the end of the day, it's just buying more stuff just for the sake of buying.

Truth be told, if we have enough to throw away, we must have enough. More often than not, we have just what we need. Let's try to see life for what it is and not what someone else tells us it should be. Let's wake up already and take a good, long look around this place. Clean out the kitchen junk drawer and donate some clothes. Realize there's more to life than buying stuff and later throwing it away. Today and going forward, let's remember what often goes forgotten…

Farm girl, you're livin' in high cotton.

Is there an area of your house you need to clean out or organize? Do you often buy things you don't need? How could you reuse or regift items? Why would it feel good to live a simpler lifestyle? What "high cotton" are you thankful for?

_____

_____

_____

_____

_____

_____

_____

_____

_____

_____

_____

_____

_____

_____

_____

_____

_____

_____

_____

"I'M livin' in HIGH COTTON."

– Holly Love King

Day 20

SING

Taking three deep breaths,
I calm my mind and body.
I welcome this moment just as it is.
It is enough, just as I am enough.

The best thing about a country road is the quiet. Most days, it's just you and the open air...and nature, of course. A wildflower here, a wildflower there. A dog barking in the distance or maybe a rooster cock-a-doodle-doo-ing. And if a neighbor happens to drive by, you'll see a wave and a nod of the head. Since we're not overpopulated, it seems people still have time for pleasantries.

I walk the same route every day, and most days a songbird joins me. She sits on a telephone wire and long before I reach her, her song greets me like a kiss. Sometimes I think she sees me and gets shy, pausing just a bit. But before you know it, she can't help herself and gets right back to the set. It's clear she's not singing for applause or even for me. She's singing for the song to be sung.

I wonder if we could create with the same freedom. Sing like no one is listening or write like no one will read. And whether people cheer or boo, would not matter in the least. We'd create for the love of it and that would be the gift. I don't want to die with a list of regrets. I want to live life to the full. These words falling on deaf ears is not my greatest fear. It's that I never write them in the first place, all these words, about loving what I see. That is what I hold so dear.

And yet far too often, I struggle to sing like the bird. I compare and contrast and quiet my little engine that could. Convincing myself that all this writing...well, it's just not that good. But all us artists are the same. Embarrassed to say we write. Too shy to expose our art. Quieting our little creative selves, the ones buried within our own hearts.

I don't care if it's a box of crayons, a pen and paper, or a guitar and pick. Let's live like the songbird and sing. Who cares if anyone listens. If anyone reads. We're not doing this for them. We're doing this for our own needs. The truth is the world has enough celebrities to go around. Do this for you. Because you're the only you this world has ever found.

What book do you want to write? What song do you want to sing, or painting do you want to paint? How has fear stopped you in the past? Give your creativity permission to be for your own enjoyment.

"SING for the SONG to be SUNG."

– Holly Love King

Day 21

SUPERHERO

Taking three deep breaths,
I calm my mind and body.
I welcome this moment just as it is.
It is enough, just as I am enough.

Some days all I seem to do is clean the house, but it's not just from cleaning my own. I also own and operate a house cleaning business, so I clean homes all over town. And for the most part, I love it. It's allowed me a flexible work schedule so I can pick my daughter up from school, tuck her into bed at night, and be home on the weekends. For me, being a mama has always mattered most. But some days I'm up to my eyeballs in dust bunnies. Just when I make someone else's kitchen shine like the Chrysler building, I have to come home and clean my own.

Yet something has happened after all these years of cleaning. I find that when I'm out of sorts, it's my go-to solution. Worried about this or sad about that and my body is drawn to the dishes like a moth to a flame. I'll scrub those dishes like a wild woman with suds flying here and there. But halfway through, the faucet is turned down, the plates calm their clanging, and I have calmed down too. It's as if the soap bubbles wash the worry right off of me.

It's not just me that feels better after a good scrubbing though. Everyone seems to benefit when the clutter and chaos are cleaned up a bit. Piles of laundry and stacks of dirty dishes for days on end are not the recipe for a calm inner state of mind. When peace and order are restored, the same can be said of our well-being and everyone is happier to be home.

No one should live like Cinderella, but when it's time to tidy up the house, don't get overwhelmed. Clean one room at a time or focus on one chore until it's done. Don't kill yourself or try to do it all in one day. Pick things up for the sake of peace, not perfection. Your house is meant to be a home, not a museum.

We may not wear a cape or a mask or save damsels in distress, but we save our sanity and our family's sanity too. As it turns out, doing the dishes is our superpower, because behind the soap suds and spray bottles, we really are happy home superheroes.

When you make your bed or clean the house, how do you feel afterward? If you struggle to stay on top of the mess, try setting small goals. In what ways would you like to create a more orderly, calm environment? Write down housekeeping goals or needs you have. If you need help from a spouse, child, or a professional house cleaner, ask! Even a superhero knows when to call for backup.

"A clean home is a HAPPY HOME."

– Unknown

Day 22

CONNECT

Taking three deep breaths,
I calm my mind and body.
I welcome this moment just as it is.
It is enough, just as I am enough.

I'm not saying I want to live on a compound or be surrounded moment-by-moment with people; I'm just saying I'm not sure humans thrive living in a castle on a hill. When you think back to how we used to live 100 or even 200 years ago, you can quickly see how fast we have evolved. Since the beginning of time, humans have needed each other for survival. If we wanted to eat, we had to hunt together. If we wanted to harvest crops, we needed to share seeds and knowledge. If we wanted to have a roof over our heads, clothes on our backs, or food on our plates, it only happened because we were doing it together.

But nowadays, we can easily go days—no, weeks— without the "need" for another human being. We can grab dinner in the drive through, buy clothes cheaper than we can sew them, and for many of us, never need the warmth of an open fire. We have HVACS for all that now. Just like we have grocery stores instead of hunting and gathering. Or we go to the mall instead of sitting around a circle of women to sew clothes or make clay pots. If we want to know how so-and-so is doing, we don't even call them. We pick up our phones and check social media. In a few seconds we can know what they did, where they are, or who they're dating… all without ever even talking to them. We put the phone down and somehow are supposed to feel "connected."

But all this social media and modern ways of living leaves us anywhere but connected. I don't know about you, but I need a good ole game night with friends or a dinner out with family to feel the warm fuzzies, not silently scrolling on my phone. I think it's safe to say, we shouldn't leave all of the past in the past. There are some things we should have never evolved out of, community and connection being at the top of that list.

We should take time to talk and look each other in the eyes. Time to smile and time to cry. Time to laugh and time to listen. Time to be together, the way humans should be. Yes, connecting with each other, whether past or present, that's the love we all really need.

What are some ways you can connect with people you love? Could you plan a girls' night out or maybe a game night in? Who in your life would you like to spend more time with? Make connecting with them a priority and feel the love.

"All you need is LOVE."

– John Lennon

Day 23

ANSWERED PRAYER

Taking three deep breaths,
I calm my mind and body.
I welcome this moment just as it is.
It is enough, just as I am enough.

Most mothers get pets for their children. Most mothers complain and go on and on about how they get stuck feeding and watering or taking them to the vet. But from the time I could walk, you could find me outside with the animals. And as an adult, I've remained pretty much the same. In love with all things furry or feathered, well, with the exception of mice. Which proved to be quite the challenge when we decided to pack up and move to the country.

The fear and reality of a mouse about the house was no joke or laughing matter for us suburban city-folk. Sure, we had laid out all the little traps, but what we needed was a cat. The only problem was my husband didn't like them. I ignored all that, decided to save myself instead and began praying to the heavens above for a cat.

After about a week of praying, a meow was heard just outside the garage in our shrubs. It was a black and gray and white little cat. My husband rolled his eyes as I quickly brought out a can of tuna. I could not believe my prayers had been answered! He was so starved for both food and affection, he couldn't decide if he wanted to eat or be held. We took him to the vet, picked out a collar, and named him Poppy. And while my husband had to get used to the idea, slowly he accepted him and even let him nap inside the house.

Poppy has proven to be worth his weight in gold. He earns his keep and then some. I've never lived in the country before but one thing I now know...mice love the country as much I do. The stories I could tell about what the cat drug in would go on for days. One time, he even brought a baby bunny in the house! Screams could be heard for miles as we yelled "drop it" and tried to save the still living, traumatized, hopping bunny.

Yes, one thing is for sure: you can't live in the country without a cat. First off, there really are a lot of little critters out there. But most of all, it's because this stray cat that showed up out of nowhere is a living, breathing answered prayer. Yes, for me, Poppy is my daily reminder that God still cares.

What are some of your answered prayers? How are these reminders that God still cares for you? Is there something now, you need to pray for? Do you ever hesitate to pray for what you want or need because you fear it won't be answered in the way you expect?

"Some prayers are answered with a meow."

– Holly Love King

Day 24

SOW

Taking three deep breaths,
I calm my mind and body.
I welcome this moment just as it is.
It is enough, just as I am enough.

If there's one lesson we farm girls know, it's that you can't reap what you don't sow. You may want a homegrown tomato come Summer, but if you don't plan for it by Spring you can kiss your fried green tomatoes goodbye. The same is true for anything worth doing. Good things come to those who wait and to those who sow. Farm life is not for the faint of heart or weary of work. You learn the hard way that if you're not willing to put in the work, the harvest season will come and go without you.

In fact, it's in the garden, tending the weeds, or plucking the ripened fruit that life's larger lessons seem to come into focus. I love growing Tithonia flowers, also known as Mexican Sunflowers. Instead of cutting them for the vase, I deadhead them so they will burst with blooms. They attract butterflies, bees, and hummingbirds like nobody's business, so I save them for the pollinators. One day while deadheading, I was having a hard time finding the dead blossoms. Right when I thought I had clipped them all, I'd find five more.

All I could think was how similar this felt to my life. Right when I tend to one part, another area needs pruning. But even more, how often I miss the "dead blossoms" still hanging on my vine. It's as if the dead hide right alongside the living, lurking in the background. As I clipped away, I thought about the shame that likes to stick or the worry I seem to wear. My own thoughts need daily pruning too, just like these dead blossoms.

That's part of why meditation has healed me. I know it helps me slow down and see. Take a good long look at the flowers growing or not growing within me. It's taught me to watch my thoughts instead of thinking I am my thoughts. And helped me harvest a life full of love that I didn't even realize I was planting. It's true, you can't reap what you don't sow. But life only gets better, when you make time to be pruned and take the risk to grow.

Does the garden teach you about life lessons too? What seeds of love do you need to plant in your life, marriage, or other relationships? How has meditation, journaling, or self-care practices helped you reap a life you love? What do you hope to harvest from living a more simple, contemplative lifestyle?

"Sow seeds of Love."

– Unknown

Day 25

CHOCOLATE GRAVY

Taking three deep breaths,
I calm my mind and body.
I welcome this moment just as it is.
It is enough, just as I am enough.

Sitting at my Grandmommy's kitchen table, she asked, "I've never made it for you before?" "No, I'd remember that for sure if you had," I answered. "It sounds weird. I can't imagine chocolate being good on a biscuit," I continued. "Well, you've never had it. Don't you knock it till you try it. I grew up eating it," Grandmommy explained. Not only did I try it, I loved it. And from then on, I grew up eating it too. Biscuits and chocolate gravy with my Grandmommy. Nothin' better.

Grandmommy had a sweet way about her. While always busy, she also had a slowness about her pace. She took time to quilt and time to teach me how to hand sew too. Time to shuck the corn and snap the beans. Even time to keep me when I was sick. Those were my favorite! The Price is Right with pancakes and Soap Operas by noon. I absolutely loved sick days! Yes, life was never too chaotic for cookies or too busy to bake. Somehow, someway, she always found time to kiss me from the kitchen.

She even had a little special kiss she'd give me right on the forehead or sometimes even a nuzzle of my nose. She'd pull me in close, a soft little smile, a wrinkle of her nose and whisper, "You little stinker, I love you." "I love you too, Grandmommy," I'd respond, wrinkling my nose just the same. It's the lingering image I hold, these years I have left to live without her. It's what keeps us together, until we share it again.

We never know what memory will last. What legacy we will leave. Sure, we try but it's not up to us what others hold dear. Will it be our donations? Maybe our goodwill? Grandmommy did many kind gestures, I can assure you. Gestures both grand and small. But as it turns out, it's chocolate gravy and kisses that mattered most of all.

So, occasionally on a weekend, you'll hear my children say, "Pass the chocolate gravy, please." Quietly I smile and even for a moment, miss. But deep down I know, Grandmommy's still loving me from the kitchen and sending me a kiss.

Take 1-2 minutes of silence and remember all the things you love about your grandparent(s). You can use the space to write them a note. Thank them or tell them how you feel. What traditions did they pass on? What traditions do you want to pass on? Treasure your loved one, knowing they are always with you.

"Life's short PASS the chocolate gravy"

— Holly Love King

Day 26

LAUGH

Taking three deep breaths,
I calm my mind and body.
I welcome this moment just as it is.
It is enough, just as I am enough.

I convinced my husband everything would be fine. I could totally paint our brick home by myself. We didn't need to hire professionals. All I needed was the white paint and a brush. Besides, we had a paint spray gun, so how hard could it be? The only problem was the spray gun began to jam. Then, the peaks of the house required scaffolding. Eventually, my wrist felt numb from so much hand painting. Until finally, I began channeling my inner Diane Keeton from the movie Baby Boom. You know the scene where the well dries up and she screams at the top of her lungs before passing out in the snow? Well, that was me, but instead of snow it was white paint. My hair was white, my glasses were white, my entire body was nothing but white paint. And I had had it! What was I thinking? Even more, what was my husband thinking? I began blaming him for not talking me out of this insane idea (Of course, all my mistakes are his fault in the middle of a meltdown).

My husband pried the paint brush from my hand and finished the job before I could do any real damage and pretty soon, we were both laughing. What in the world had ever made me think I could do this? Paint the outside of our house by myself? By hand? Climbing up and down scaffolding? For over a month?! That is the recipe for a meltdown! And a belly full of laughter.

I'm not sure why I convince myself or anyone else of my hair brained ideas. No, this was not my first and would not be my last. But regardless of my lack of forethought, this way of living does produce ample laughter and I've come to learn life is not worth living if you can't laugh at it. Far too often, we grown-ups find it easier to grumble than grin. We take life too seriously and see mistakes as personal failure. But life should be fun, adventurous, and free. We should live like big kids instead of grumpy old men. And while I've learned I don't need to paint a house by myself, I've also learned:

Life's much more fun, if you can laugh at yourself.

Laughter is the best medicine so choose a funny movie or show to watch. If you need help choosing, *Baby Boom* is a good one. Use the space below to write down some of your funniest memories and have a good laugh.

_____

_____

_____

_____

_____

_____

_____

_____

_____

_____

_____

_____

_____

_____

_____

_____

_____

_____

_____

_____

"Life is better when you're laughing."

- Unknown

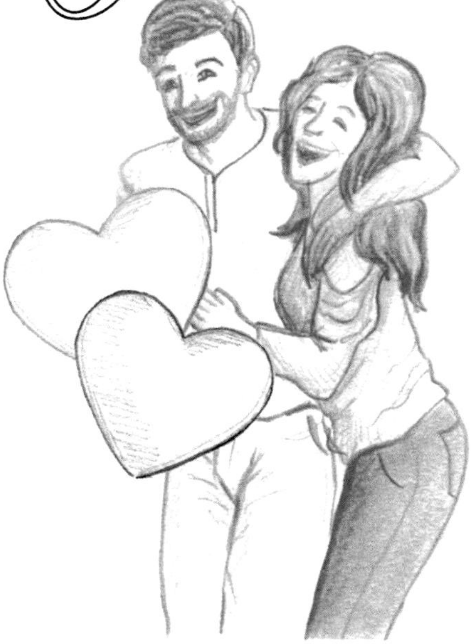

Day 27

HELD

Taking three deep breaths,
I calm my mind and body.
I welcome this moment just as it is.
It is enough, just as I am enough.

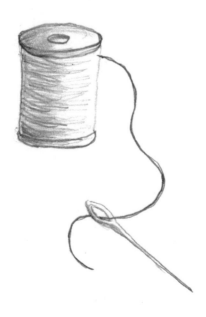

I've heard the saying that sewing is cheaper than therapy and I can't say I disagree. At times, it seemed to be the only thing holding me together during the COVID-19 pandemic. Too much news, too much fear, too much stress, and way too much time on our hands left me in search of anything to do. And I found it through embroidery. Praise Jesus!

I was well on my way into a new kind-of heaven when I realized I was also well on my way to becoming a floss and fabric hoarder. Planning new projects before the first one was finished. Running to the store for one color of floss only to leave with five others. Seeing this new pattern or that cute design. Loving all I was learning and even more, all I was stitching. Each night, as my family watched TV, my daughter, Scout, and I would hold our hoops in hand, and almost like taking a step back in time, get lost in needle and thread.

This lost art began to quiet my mind and soothe my soul. It was lighting new creative sparks and doing more than distracting. It was bringing out something new and reconnecting me to the past all at the same time. I could see how our hurried lives had run right by this slow and steady practice. Screens and scrolling seem more exciting, or at least more important that stitching and sewing. But whether we're living with the pandemic or the predictable, the truth is we don't need hours and hours of news or social media. We need space to hear and quiet to calm. We need the off button and the mute one too.

We're made for much more than stress and worry. We're made to hunt and gather. Live together and share. Yes, I learned a lot by slowing down. I learned there's more to life than spinning fast and buying all I see. More than news or TV. There's time for craft and time to create. And it does much more than avoid the things I dread. Looking down at my hoop, it was clear to see, I was being held together by a needle and a thread.

Do you enjoy sewing, embroidery, or needle work? If not, consider giving one a try. It is reported that sewing can increase brain cell growth since it requires creativity and is said to increase dopamine levels causing you to feel happier. Use the space below to journal things you learned during the COVID-19 pandemic and/or things that helped you cope.

_____

_____

_____

_____

_____

_____

_____

_____

_____

_____

_____

_____

_____

_____

_____

_____

_____

_____

"I am held together by a needle and a thread."

— Holly Love King

Day 28

SACRED BATHTUB

Taking three deep breaths,
I calm my mind and body.
I welcome this moment just as it is.
It is enough, just as I am enough.

I know a house needs a kitchen and table, bathroom and bedroom, but I also know my house is not a home without a little nook made just for me. A place to get away and get quiet. A place I can meditate and breathe, journal or be one with the silence. It doesn't have to be fancy or even its own separate room. Just a little space to call my own and calm my mind is all I need.

Some people like to burn incense, sit on a pillow and close their eyes to meditate. Others find it helpful to set a timer or listen to chimes. There are apps on your phone to help you slow down and become more mindful. Countless scientific studies prove the benefits of meditation. There's no denying in our growing technological world, the need to unplug and unwind only grows too.

For my meditation I don't sit cross legged on a pillow or even a hay bale ☺. I don't close my eyes or burn incense. It's not that I disagree, they're just not my "jam". I like to sit on a comfy chair or couch with my journal and pen. I call it my "quiet time" and almost always make it happen in the morning. I turn off my phone, grab my coffee, and quiet my thoughts through writing. I dump out the day on paper and then listen to the silence once I'm done. Positive thoughts seem free to float to the top after I've gotten my chattering mind out of the way. I write down my worries or questions or even some new ideas and calm, loving, reassuring thoughts will come to mind. I write down what I "hear" and feel put back together, whole, and made new. It's like I wash off the world and put me back on.

For as many people as there are in the world, there are just as many ways to meditate. The method is not what matters. Reclaiming our minds and growing positive thoughts is the point. But a little haven in your very own home sure does help. Find a spot in your closet, patio, or convert a laundry room or attic. It's not about finding another place to decorate and adorn or even some small little nook to create. This is your holy ground, a "sacred bathtub" if you will. A place to wash off the world and put you, the real you, back on.

Where in your house can you go to get away? Think of creative ways to find a spot just for you. Keep the space simple and calming but also filled with things that you love. If you're short on space, consider a closet or even just a special throw pillow or candle you can bring out during your meditation time. This will help signal your brain that it's time for YOU.

"Wash off the world and put YOU back on."

— Holly Love King

FOUNDATION

Taking three deep breaths,
I calm my mind and body.
I welcome this moment just as it is.
It is enough, just as I am enough.

On occasion, we eat dinner in front of the TV. It can be nice to watch a show and let the day unwind while you eat. However, most nights we eat dinner together at the table. I love setting out the white plates and cloth napkins, the fancy water glasses too. It's not that I need the pomp and circumstance of fine dining, but rather the warm fuzzies from being together. I know these years when the kids are young will go by fast, too many already have. So, when we're all home I like to make it special.

When the kids were little, we'd play trivia games to distract picky eaters and avoid meltdowns. We also used to sing the prayer instead of saying it. My stepson, Braden, who was three years old at the time, thought Amen was pronounced, "awe man". So, for a few years we all said, "awe man" at the end of every prayer and loved it. Other times, we've cleared the dishes and set up a board game right after the meal. But no matter what age or stage, there are some things that seem to stick like glue. Like, holding hands when we pray, or clinking our cups as we all say "cheers!" Talking about the day, what went well or what did not. Hearing about school, sports, friends, and work seem to be just as predictable as the plates we eat on. And at some point, my husband will almost always place his hand on my leg under the table.

Dinner time is for feeding my kids their fruits and veggies, and even my husband too. I want to model healthy habits and polite manners, but I've learned eating together does much more. Most days, we're all going in different directions. Different schedules and agendas. Unique lives with individual dreams. But the table brings us back together and these are the moments I cherish the most. The little everyday things that in the end, always add up to a whole lot.

Don't get me wrong, I still love vacations and big holiday traditions. We love to surprise our kids with fun little treats. And our marriage thrives on twice-a-month date nights. Those special moments are much needed, for sure. But I know the real foundation keeping us stable, is best found at our kitchen table.

Make mealtime at the table a priority. Look those you love in the eyes and get to know them better. Set out some special dishes or light a candle. Buy a dinner time trivia game and have fun. If you can't eat every meal with someone you care for, choose one or two days a week when you can and make it count. No cell phones allowed. Write down what you love about eating meals with friends and family and plan your next dinner date!

_____

_____

_____

_____

_____

_____

_____

_____

_____

_____

_____

_____

_____

_____

_____

_____

_____

_____

"Dinner is better when we EAT TOGETHER."

– Unknown

Day 30

NEED

Taking three deep breaths,
I calm my mind and body.
I welcome this moment just as it is.
It is enough, just as I am enough.

I never knew I'd need a stump grinder, wheelbarrow, or tractor, but living in the country has a way of a helping you become a bit needy. Planted smack dab in the middle of nowhere and you're soon on the lookout for other life forms. We longed for a little more solitude but in no way wanted isolation either. So, having two neighbors within walking distance was a nice balance for our new country life. Later however, we came to find out that if you live within ten miles of each other you're considered neighbors and that was fine by me. As long as we had space to breath, the more the merrier.

One of the first things our country house needed was a fence for our dog, Pumpkin. The only problem was a huge tree stump right in the way of the fence line. I must have called ten different tree services and finally found one that could fit me in the upcoming weekend. He said he'd swing by on Saturday because he was our neighbor and lived right up the road. Sure enough, he was there on Saturday grinding the stump and pretty soon, his wife and daughter joined him. We met as neighbors but parted as friends.

A few weekends later while cleaning up the overgrown shrubs, I needed a wheelbarrow and had one to borrow after meeting the neighbors across the street. Come Spring, I needed a full-on tractor to move mounds and mounds of wood chips to the garden. I was making do with a shovel and our newly purchased wheelbarrow when the other walking-distance neighbor took pity on me. He offered his services and tractor and soon I renamed him my Tractor Cowboy. A few years into this country life and I found myself in need again, but this time for an editor. I had farm girl stories bubbling up in me like the spring near my house. And as it turns out, Tractor Cowboy's better half is an editor! What were the chances?!

Before moving here, I don't think I ever borrowed much more than a cup of sugar. I sure never needed a tractor, wheelbarrow, or stump grinder. But what matters is not the stuff a neighbor can lend, but the way it can turn a nice neighbor into a good friend.

Make a list of neighbors you are thankful for. What have they done to help you or how have they made your life better? When you are in need do you ask for help or struggle to reach out? What are some ways you could meet or get to know your neighbors better? In what ways could you help them?

_____

_____

_____

_____

_____

_____

_____

_____

_____

_____

_____

_____

_____

_____

_____

_____

_____

_____

"Won't you be my neighbor?"

— Mister Rogers

Day 31

HAY BALE

Taking three deep breaths,
I calm my mind and body.
I welcome this moment just as it is.
It is enough, just as I am enough.

Sometimes I cannot believe it has taken me nearly half a century to feel good. It's not that I was born with a debilitating disease or some chronic physical illness, but my life, at least the first 30 some years, has had its fair share of emotional pain. It seems it has been my life's mission to quite literally save myself from the hurt I felt within. And although I could have a doctorate degree in emotional healing, some days I still feel shocked that I feel good. A deep, down to the bone-marrow, gut-level good.

But all this feeling good didn't get here overnight. From reading books, to seeking counseling, and finding friends that could relate, I have tried it all. I didn't wake up yesterday and decide to write a book about meditative thoughts. There's a reason I'm writing this book, and it's because I know the work it takes to emotionally heal. I've healed from my parents' divorce and later, my own. Being a pregnant teenager and placing my son for open adoption. Making mistakes and thinking I was a mistake too. Getting remarried and the hard work it takes to "blend". Healed and whole became my new normal and I threw the rest right out the window.

Yet, in the mist of all those ups and downs, most days looked as commonplace as the grass. So normal and ordinary they feel like nothing at all. For some reason though, it seems we focus on the "hay bales" of life. But there's more to life than the bumps. There's calm routines and peaceful mornings. Quiet cups of coffee and singing in the car. Dishes washed and put away. Laundry folded and saying your prayers. Hands that you've held and others that have held you too. Yes, these are the real makings of our days.

The truth is, this too shall pass, and all things have a way of working together for good. Farm Girl, take it from me, your fellow wounded-friend, you're not a mistake and you're more than your problems. All these days you're living, those you label "pass" and still others "fail"… trust me, all we're ever really doing is floating on a hay bale.

Looking back, can you see how things you first labeled "bad" worked out as good? How have the hard things in your life ended up making life easier or better for you or your family? In what ways have you grown from the "hay bales" of life? Next time you face a challenging life situation, refuse to label it bad or hard. Instead, envision yourself floating on top of the situation until it passes.

"I'm floating on a hay bale."

- Holly Love King

Acknowledgements

Brad: Thank you for your willingness to go on new adventures with me. And your patience as I sample one of every creative spark I have and then ask you to help make it happen. I love being your baby. And I love that you are mine.

Andrew, Scout, and Braden: Thank you for letting me share your stories. I love that our stories are written together. You are the beats of my heart and the three cherries on top of my life.

Mom: Little did we know your subscription gift to Mary Jane's Farm Magazine would lead me all the way here. From the first poem I showed you in middle school, to my first story published in my forties, thank you for being just as excited as I am. It means the world to me. I love you.

Rhonda Poole: Thank you for taking so much time, attention, and care to my words. These pages are made better because you have been in them. Thank you for teaching me but also for cheering me on my way. Not only are you an amazing editor, but also friend and neighbor. My little engine that could chugs a bit stronger now because of you.

Mary Jane's Farm Magazine: Thank you for choosing to publish my stories in your beautiful magazine. For teaching me that "Farm Girl" is a state of mind, not where you live. For being THE inspiration that sprouted this book...that hopefully will sprout meditating Farm Girls everywhere!

Elizabeth King Design: Thank you for your vision of this book. Your creative touches make this little book ooze with joy. Sprinkles of paw prints and boquets of wildflowers make us want to bust out the ole' crayons and color. Thank you, Liz.

Holly is a freelance writer and author. She loves being with her family and is happiest when she is home—in a fixer-upper on 5 acres off a country road in Tennessee...living her dream come true. Learn more at IG @ farmgirlmeditations

Emily Wright (AHKI) is an artist / illustrator who works primarily in graphite pencil, yet sometimes dabbles in paints and colour when the time is right. Having completed a Bachelor of Illustration and established herself as an exhibiting artist in Melbourne, Emily is now currently living and working on the beautiful Surf Coast of Victoria, AU.

Predominantly Emily's works centre around the natural world, and all of its living inhabitants; a direct reflection of Emily's own love of nature and the outdoors. Emily surrounds herself with other local and Melbourne based artists, musicians, and creatives to keep herself inspired and constantly motivated. Learn more at ahkiillustration.wixsite.com/ahki or IG @ahki_illustration

Kevin Faulkner is a freelance artist and graphic designer who works in all mediums from graphite to digital. He has a degree in graphic design with a focus in illustration from Middle Tennessee State University. He works and operates throughout middle tennessee and is always happy to go explore and find inspiration from the beauty that's all around. Learn more at IG @wonderedbliss

Made in the USA
Las Vegas, NV
21 December 2022

63678859R00083